Polar Bears

by Rebecca Pettiford

BELLWETHER MEDIA • MINNEAPOLIS, MN

BLASTOFF!
READERS
2

Note to Librarians, Teachers, and Parents:

Blastoff! Readers are carefully developed by literacy experts and combine standards-based content with developmentally appropriate text.

Level 1 provides the most support through repetition of high-frequency words, light text, predictable sentence patterns, and strong visual support.

Level 2 offers early readers a bit more challenge through varied simple sentences, increased text load, and less repetition of high-frequency words.

Level 3 advances early-fluent readers toward fluency through increased text and concept load, less reliance on visuals, longer sentences, and more literary language.

Level 4 builds reading stamina by providing more text per page, increased use of punctuation, greater variation in sentence patterns, and increasingly challenging vocabulary.

Level 5 encourages children to move from "learning to read" to "reading to learn" by providing even more text, varied writing styles, and less familiar topics.

Whichever book is right for your reader, Blastoff! Readers are the perfect books to build confidence and encourage a love of reading that will last a lifetime!

This edition first published in 2019 by Bellwether Media, Inc.

No part of this publication may be reproduced in whole or in part without written permission of the publisher. For information regarding permission, write to Bellwether Media, Inc., Attention: Permissions Department, 6012 Blue Circle Drive, Minnetonka, MN 55343.

Library of Congress Cataloging-in-Publication Data

Names: Pettiford, Rebecca, author.
Title: Polar Bears / by Rebecca Pettiford.
Description: Minneapolis, MN : Bellwether Media, Inc., 2019. |
   Series: Blastoff! Readers. Animals of the Arctic | Audience: Age 5-8. |
   Audience: K to Grade 3. | Includes bibliographical references and index.
Identifiers: LCCN 2018030953 (print) | LCCN 2018036177 (ebook) |
   ISBN 9781681036632 (ebook) | ISBN 9781626179387 (hardcover : alk. paper)
Subjects: LCSH: Polar bear--Juvenile literature. | Animals--Arctic regions--Juvenile literature.
Classification: LCC QL737.C27 (ebook) | LCC QL737.C27 P429 2019 (print) | DDC 599.786--dc23
LC record available at https://lccn.loc.gov/2018030953

Text copyright © 2019 by Bellwether Media, Inc. BLASTOFF! READERS and associated logos are trademarks and/or registered trademarks of Bellwether Media, Inc. SCHOLASTIC, CHILDREN'S PRESS, and associated logos are trademarks and/or registered trademarks of Scholastic Inc., 557 Broadway, New York, NY 10012.

Editor: Rebecca Sabelko   Designer: Jeffrey Kollock

Printed in the United States of America, North Mankato, MN

Table of Contents

Life in the Arctic

Polar bears are the world's largest land **carnivores**! They live on sea ice and the frozen Arctic **tundra**.

These great white bears have **adapted** to make this **biome** their home!

Polar Bear Range

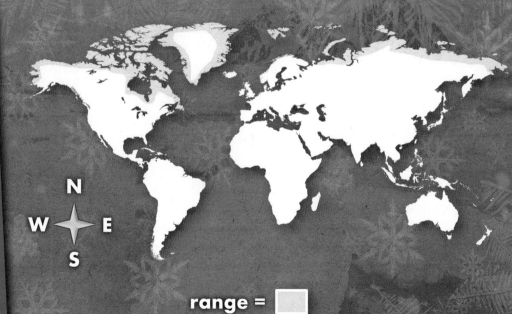

N
W · E
S

range = ▢

Polar bears have black skin.
Their skin takes in heat.
Two thick layers of fur trap heat.

black skin

Blubber under their skin
also keeps the bears warm.

padded foot

Polar bears have big,
padded feet for walking
on snow and sea ice.

Small bumps on the bottom of their feet keep them from sliding on ice.

Clean Swimmers

Staying clean and dry keeps polar bears warm.

They bathe in open water. They lick their feet. Then, they shake the water from their fur.

Polar Bear Stats

Least Concern	Near Threatened	Vulnerable	Endangered	Critically Endangered	Extinct in the Wild	Extinct

conservation status: vulnerable

life span: 25 years

Polar bears can swim for many hours to find food.

Special Adaptations

black skin

large, padded feet

webbed toes

They paddle using their **webbed** front toes.
They steer with their back feet.

Seals are polar bears' favorite food. These bears spend hours waiting by seal breathing holes.

When seals take a breath, the bears strike!

A Melting Hunting Ground

Polar bears mostly eat
the blubber of ringed seals.

They can eat 100 pounds (45 kilograms) of blubber in one meal!

When seals are hard to find, polar bears walk the rocky shores looking for food.

18

They eat seabirds
and beached whales.
They will even eat garbage!

Polar Bear Diet

ringed seals

bearded seals

beluga whales

Climate change is causing polar bears' icy home to melt.

But their many adaptations
help them stay afloat!

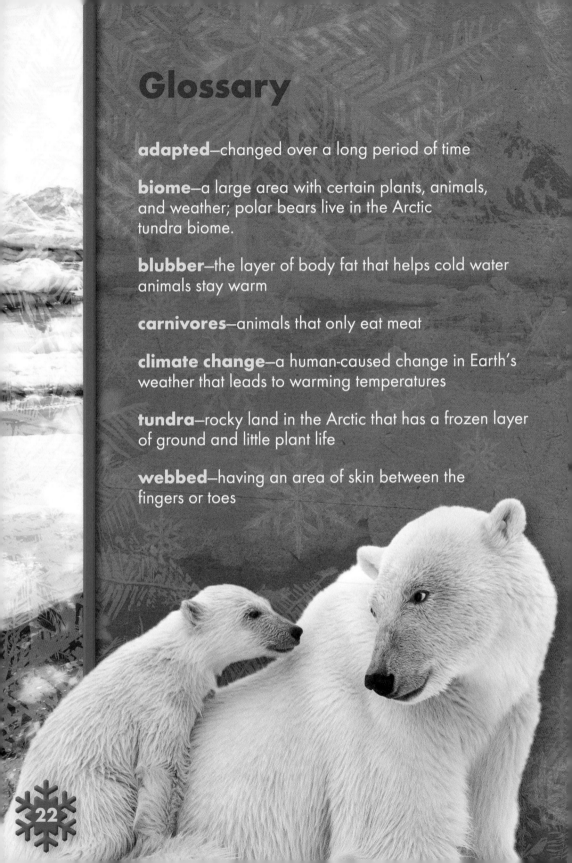

Glossary

adapted—changed over a long period of time

biome—a large area with certain plants, animals, and weather; polar bears live in the Arctic tundra biome.

blubber—the layer of body fat that helps cold water animals stay warm

carnivores—animals that only eat meat

climate change—a human-caused change in Earth's weather that leads to warming temperatures

tundra—rocky land in the Arctic that has a frozen layer of ground and little plant life

webbed—having an area of skin between the fingers or toes

To Learn More

AT THE LIBRARY

Carrington, Stephanie. *Huge Polar Bears.* New York, N.Y.: Gareth Stevens Publishing, 2018.

Gillespie, Katie. *A Polar Bear's World.* New York, N.Y.: AV2 by Weigl, 2018.

Ripley, Mark. *How Do Polar Bears Stay Warm?* New York, N.Y.: PowerKids Press, 2017.

ON THE WEB

FACTSURFER

Factsurfer.com gives you a safe, fun way to find more information.

1. Go to www.factsurfer.com.

2. Enter "polar bears" into the search box.

3. Click the "Surf" button and select your book cover to see a list of related web sites.

Index

The images in this book are reproduced through the courtesy of: Iakov Filimonov, front cover (polar bear); Incredible Arctic, pp. 4-5; Baranov E, p. 6; outdoorsman, pp. 6-7; Don Land, pp. 8-9; Heather M. Davidson, p. 8 (bubble); Jo Crebin, p. 9; Riekus, p. 10; Frand Hildebrand/ Getty, pp. 10-11; Caleb Foster, pp. 12-13; FloridaStock, pp. 13, 14-15; NoDerog, p. 13 (bubble); Storimages, p. 14; Chase Dekker, pp. 16-17; Ondrej Prosicky, pp. 17, 19 (bearded seal), 20; Vladimir Melnik, pp. 18-19; polarman, p. 19 (ringed seal); Miles Away Photography, p. 19 (beluga whale); Andre Anita, pp. 20-21; Gecko1968, p. 22.